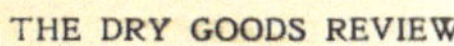

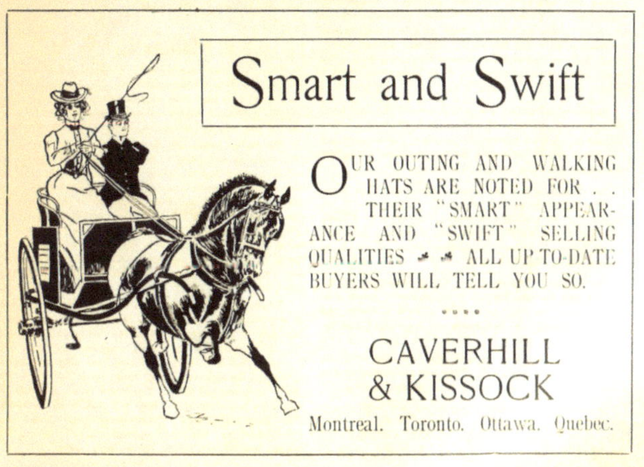

Vintage Dry Goods Catalog Pages
By C. Anders

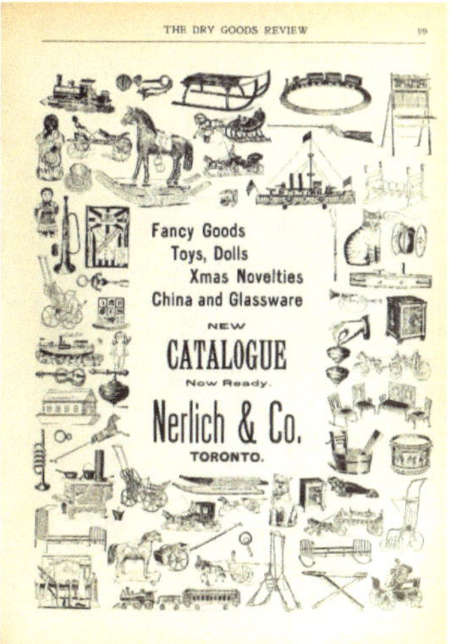

MILLINERY OPENING

Monday, Tuesday, Wednesday and following Days

29TH FEBRUARY, 1ST AND 2ND MARCH

** The Trade invited to call and inspect the largest and best assorted Stock in the Dominion.

D. McCALL & CO.

Wholesale Millinery Importers

1831 NOTRE DAME ST.,
MONTREAL

12 AND 14 WELLINGTON ST. EAST,
TORONTO

always opens with a new color. This year it is known as "Pompadour," and is a bluish green ; the second shade being known as "Watteau." Following it come the mauves, the most delicate of which is known as "Eglantine." A large number are ambers in three shades headed by "Eldorado." Next in importance are the greys in two classes, the latter known as "beiges," of a smoky hue. The impression created by the array of sixty fine colors is that of a prevalent quietness and delicacy in pale blue, soft yellow, and clear grey.

A QUESTION OF PRIVILEGE.

Mrs. O'Hara—That's a foine way fur a man t' go dhownshtairs ! Mr. O'Hara—Can't a man go dhownshtairs ony dom way he plazes ?

The new Dominion Veiling, the latest novelty.

We have much pleasure in calling the attention of the trade to the advertisement of Perrin Freres & Cie on page 32, who are celebrated the world over for their gloves.

jet and osprey aigrettes of the Mephisto order, which are one of the latest novelties in the feather and ornament line. The narrow ties are of black velvet ribbon No. 7.

FIG. 2.

FIG. 3.

Mr. Hurst, a well-known traveller formerly with C. M. Taylor & Co., is one of the firm of Morton, Densen & Hurst, who are selling an automatic counter-check book. This book is patented by these gentlemen in Canada, and as no carbon leaf is necessary to produce the impression, it is much superior to carbon leaf books. The prices are also slightly lower than the older styles of counter check books, and hence has an additional advantage. The firms advertisement may be found in another column.

Messrs. Alexander & Anderson are at present showing a very complete line of dress goods, consisting of new effects in dress tweeds, homespun and Harris suitings, and a full assortment of French and German dress goods, robes, etc. This department is a special feature of this house and worthy of the attention of visiting merchants. In cloakings they are showing all the latest novelties in mantle cloths, ulsterings, curls, sealettes, etc.

FIG 4.

WYLD, GRASETT & DARLING.

Our Importations for the Fall Trade are of the most comprehensive character, and inspection of the same by all Independent Dry Goods Merchants and Merchant Tailors' is solicited.

Canadian Staples AT THE Lowest Quotations

TRAVELLERS' AND LETTER ORDERS PROMPTLY SHIPPED.

WYLD, GRASETT & DARLING.

SUSPENDERS.

We want to get everybody using the **V** make of Suspenders, and then every dealer will be selling them. In order to do this we turn out only first class goods, both in material and workmanship. See our samples.

C. N. VROOM,

St. Stephen, N.B.

GOULDING & CO., 27 Wellington St. East, Toronto.

Agents for Ontario.

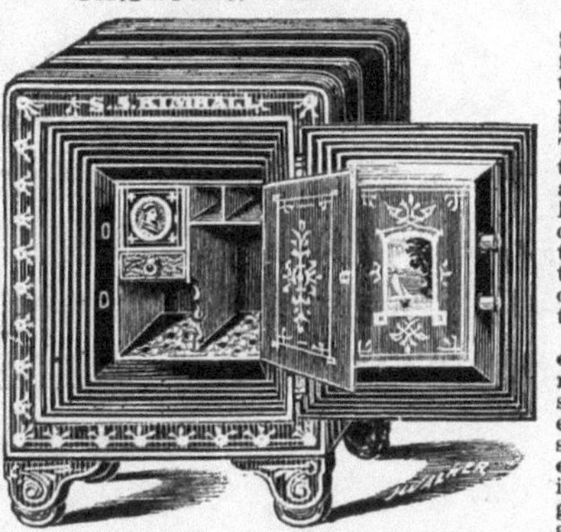

CHAMPION FIRE AND BURGLAR-PROOF SAFES.

If you are in need of a Safe it will pay you to write for catalogue or call and see them; twelve years' use have proved them to be the best Safe made for the money. There has never been one of them opened by a burglar, although many attempts have been made on them. I can show where over fifty of them have been in some of the worst fires, and no one can show a cent's damage to any of their contents. **Our prices are much lower than other good safes. We manufacture them all ourselves, and while other makers pay 25 per cent. commission for selling, we sell direct to the user, thereby saving that much.** Catalogue giving size, prices, etc., on application.

CHAMPION CASH AND PARCEL CARRIER.

The advantages of this Carrier are many over any other. First, it has a cup that does not take off, therefore it does not get mislaid or fall and scatter the change. The cup is the size to take a bill without folding, making it easier for the cashier and saving time.

The wheels are large and it runs easy without noise.

The price is lower than any first-class Carrier. It has been in use for over a year in many of the largest stores in the Dominion, and in every case has given the best of satisfaction.

Send for circular giving all particulars.

S. S. KIMBALL, MANUFACTURER - - - 577 CRAIG STREET, **MONTREAL.**

Bell Pianos.

THE BEST THAT CAN BE PRODUCED.

Are the choice of the musical profession everywhere for Full Rich Tone, Substantial Construction and Elegant Appearance.

Send for Catalogue to THE BELL ORGAN AND PIANO CO., Ltd., Guelph, Ont.

BRANCH WAREROOMS:

TORONTO, ONT,	LONDON, ONT.,	HAMILTON, ONT
70 King St. West.	211 Dundas St.	44 James St. North.

We beg to inform the trade that we have now in stock a complete line of Fur and Wool, Stiff and Soft hats of the most desirable shapes, from the following manufacturers :

    Lincoln, Bennett & Co.,
       Wilkinson & Co.,
           and J. E. Mills,

and that we are in a position to fill orders for fall trade without delay.

The Fur department is receiving special attention, and we invite an inspection of our samples on the road.

B. Levin & Co.

491 and 493 ST. PAUL STREET, MONTREAL, P. Q.

— THE —

AMAZON
VELVET SKIRT FACING
A NEW FABRIC FOR BINDING SKIRTS.

ADVANTAGES :

DURABILITY—Will outwear a dozen old-fashioned braids.

NEATNESS—The Pile of the Velvet gives a smart finish to the bottom of the skirt. Being cut on the bias it does not ravel and does not injure the shoe.

ECONOMY—Being done up in continuous lengths (3 yards) sufficient for each skirt.

ALL FASHIONABLE DRESS SHADES.

MANUFACTURED BY

MEYERHOF, MARX & SIMONSEN, MANCHESTER.

Representative : FRED KING, 61 Piccadilly, Manchester.

WHOLESALE ONLY.

FALL, 1892.

A. A. ALLAN & CO.

Wholesale Furs, Hats, Caps, Gloves and Robes.

We are foremost in the race for value and styles and in each of our departments close buyers will find a great variety at attractive prices.

A. A. ALLAN & CO.,

51 Bay Street, Toronto.

BUYERS WILL DO THE RIGHT THING

When ordering **LAMA DRESS BRAID** if they order it put up in rolls and see that this label is on the cover of each box.

LISTER & CO.

(LIMITED)

Manningham Mills

BRADFORD, - - ENGLAND

(Paid up Capital, $10,000,000)

Are the Largest and most Reliable
Makers of Pile Fabrics
in the World.

Silk Seals, Silk Velvets, black and colored,
Dress and Millinery Plushes, Etc.
Silk and Mohair Furniture Plushes, Etc.

To be had of all the leading Wholesale
Houses in Canada.

SOLE AGENTS FOR THE DOMINION:

H. L. SMYTH & CO., Montreal and Toronto

SPRING 1884.
NOVELTY PATTERNS & STYLES

IN WHITE SILKS

White Grounds with Colored Embroidery
and newest shades in Colored Grounds.

Piques in all sizes of cords, styles and
qualities in white and fancy.

The latest Bow is "The York."
We have a very large range at
all prices.

E. & S. CURRIE, 64 Bay St., TORONTO.

Still a Favorite : :

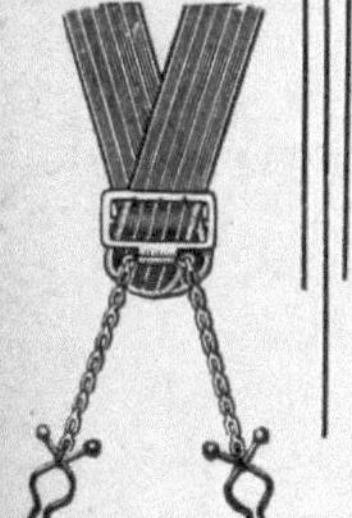

Our Reliable Suspender has sold largely
ever since we introduced it to the trade.

No Sewing to give out! No button
holes bursting! No pulling apart in the
back ! . . . .

If you haven't seen it, send 50 cents for
a sample pair.

We make a complete line of Braces,
Hose Supporters, Belts, etc., and keep up
to the times. A specially fine line of Holi-
day Braces. . . . . .

C. N. VROOM, St. Stephen, New Brunswick

¼ size fac-simile of package.

BUTTERMILK
TOILET SOAP

THE BEST SELLING TOILET
SOAP IN THE WORLD.

**Excels any 25 cent Soap on the Market.
Nets the retailer a good profit.**

**When sold at a very popular price it
will not remain on your counters. Try
a sample lot.**

The quality of this soap is GUARANTEED. See
that the name "BUTTERMILK" is printed as above
"in green bronze" and the name "Cosmo Buttermilk
Soap Company, Chicago," in diamond on end of package. Beware of Imitations.

Cosmo Buttermilk Soap Co.
84 ADAMS ST., CHICAGO

F. W. HUDSON & CO., Sole Agents, TORONTO.

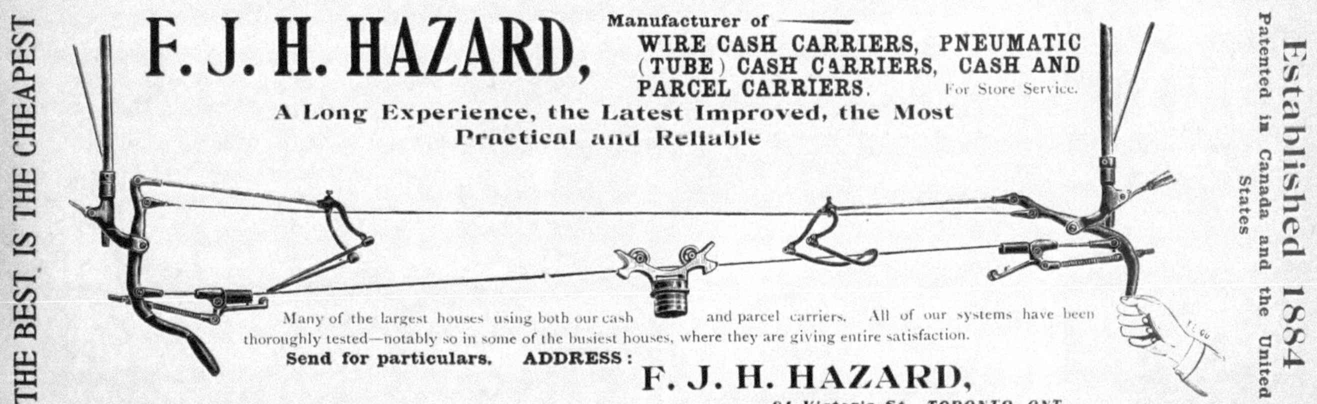

THE "TENDIMUS" SKIRT BAND

(ROUND WOVEN ELASTIC TOP.)

Made in
all Colors
and Fancy
Stripes,
$3\frac{1}{2}$ and $4\frac{1}{2}$ in.
Deep.

PERFECT
SHAPE.

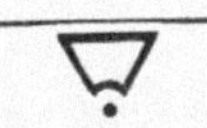

Having
an Elastic
Heading is most
Comfortable in
Wear, and the
Rubber Threads
being specially
Protected in
Weaving,
its Durability is
Guaranteed.

The "TENDIMUS" BAND is now supplied in

HANDSOME INLAID ROSEWOOD CABINETS

CONTAINING

Six Dozen

WITHOUT

Extra Charge

Also in 3 doz.
Strong Cloth
Stock Boxes.

And in the
usual 1 doz.
Cartons.

<u>Sole Agents for Canada</u>   **W. R. BROCK & CO., Toronto.**

World Wide Popularity   **The Delicious Perfume.**

Crab Apple Blossoms

EXTRA CONCENTRATED

Put up in 1, 2, 3, 4, 6, 8, and 16 ounce bottles.

And the Celebrated

Crown Lavender Salts

Annual sales exceed 500,000 bottles. Sold everywhere.

THE CROWN PERFUMERY CO.

177 New Bond St., London, Eng.

By all principal dealers in perfumery.

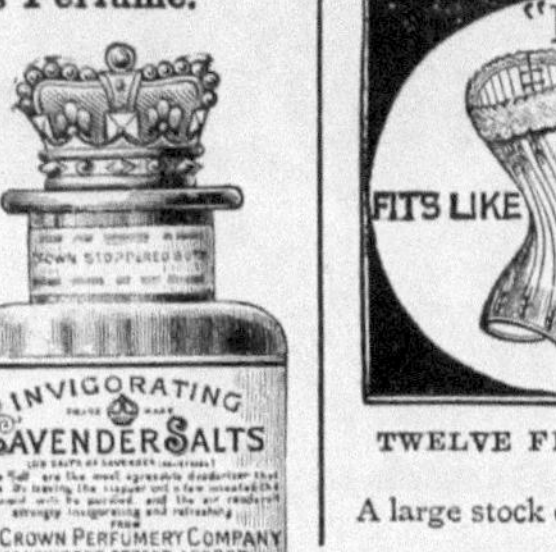

"FITS LIKE A GLOVE."

THOMSON'S

ENGLISH MADE,

Glove-Fitting. Long Waisted.   TRADE MARK.

CORSETS   At Popular Prices.

The Perfection of Shape, Finish and Durability.

APPROVED by the whole polite world.

SALE OVER ONE MILLION PAIRS ANNUALLY.

TWELVE FIRST MEDALS.

A large stock of these GOOD VALUE Corsets always on hand at

JOHN MACDONALD & CO'S, TORONTO.

MANUFACTURERS: **W. S. THOMSON & CO., LIMITED, LONDON.**

See that every Corset is marked "THOMSON'S GLOVE FITTING," and bears our Trade Mark, the Crown. No others are genuine.

Thomas Mealey & Co.

MANUFACTURERS OF

Wadded Carpet Lining

MEALEY STAIR PAD.

AND

STAIR PADS

HAMILTON, ONT.

OFFICE.—

24 Catharine St. North.

THE C. TURNBULL CO., Ltd.

OF GALT, ONT.,

MANUFACTURERS OF

Full-Finished Lambs Wool Underclothing. Ladies' Full-Fashioned Underwear in all Wool, Merino and Medium. Men's Full-Fashioned Underwear in all-Wool, Merino and Medium. Ladies', Boys' and Girls' Combination Suits, Full Fashioned. Ladies', Boys' Shirts and Drawers.

SEND FOR PRICE LIST.

THE BEST IS THE CHEAPEST

F. J. H. HAZARD,

Manufacturer of

WIRE CASH CARRIERS, PNEUMATIC (TUBE) CASH CARRIERS, CASH AND PARCEL CARRIERS. For Store Service.

A Long Experience, the Latest Improved, the Most Practical and Reliable

Established 1884

Patented in Canada and the United States

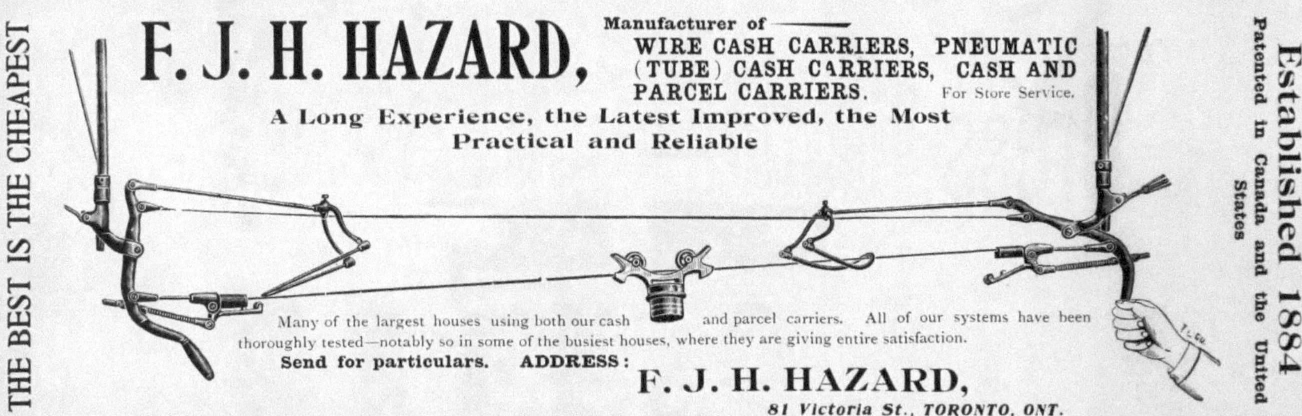

Many of the largest houses using both our cash and parcel carriers. All of our systems have been thoroughly tested—notably so in some of the busiest houses, where they are giving entire satisfaction.

Send for particulars.   ADDRESS:

F. J. H. HAZARD,

81 Victoria St., TORONTO, ONT.

DO YOU STOCK THEM?

"Maltese Cross" BRAND

Mackintoshes.

Sold by all the leading wholesale houses.   Will never grow hard.

ODORLESS, TAILOR FASHIONED, SEAMS SEWN.

. . . MANUFACTURED SOLELY BY . . .

The Gutta Percha & Rubber Mfg. Co.

of TORONTO, Ltd.

61 AND 63 FRONT STREET WEST, TORONTO.

Wyld, Grasett & Darling

SPECIAL LINES SUITABLE FOR NOVEMBER TRADE

Leading lines in Flannelettes, large ranges of patterns.

Eiderdowns, in Plain and Fancy Styles, also Napped, in Plain Colors.

Complete ranges of weights and sizes in White Union and All Wool, also Extra Super Blankets. Grey Union and All Wool Blankets. Horse Blankets. . . . . . .

Hosiery--Ladies' and Children's plain and ribbed, full range.

Ladies' and Children's Underwear in Natural Wool.

Mantlings, Beavers, Astrachans, Curls, . . . Etc.

WYLD, GRASETT & DARLING

TORONTO.

Mantles AND Jackets

THE subscribers desire to call attention to their MAGNIFICENT DISPLAY of NEW and STYLISH CREATIONS for the EARLY FALL and WINTER TRADE.

Our "PRINCESS ALIX" Combination Jacket is a pronounced success. "GOLF CAPES a specialty.

INSPECTION SOLICITED.

Alexander & Anderson

MANTLE MANUFACTURERS

TORONTO

Ready for Spring Trade

Neatness and Economy Combined.

Strength, Durability and a Novelty.

The American Fashion for . . . .

LADIES AND GENTLEMEN

We claim that for the better class of trade our "Tight Rollers" will have preference over every other style.

SAMPLES NOW ON THE ROAD

Irving & Co.

Cor. Yonge and Walton Sts.

TORONTO

MAKERS

Neckwear Novelties

For the . . . .

Holiday Trade

We are showing a large range of styles which we make in

White Cord
White Brocade
And
Light Fancies

Especially designed for the

CHRISTMAS TRADE

E. & S. CURRIE

64 BAY ST.
TORONTO

THERE'S NO **?** ABOUT IT.

The New
Silk Stitched

EVER-READY DRESS STAYS

—— ARE THE ONLY ——

Desirable Substitute for Whalebone Obtainable

Let us prove it by sending you samples

Don't compel a customer to enforce her demand in this manner, but order

*

MADE IN SATTEEN, RIBBON CLOTH AND SATIN

❋

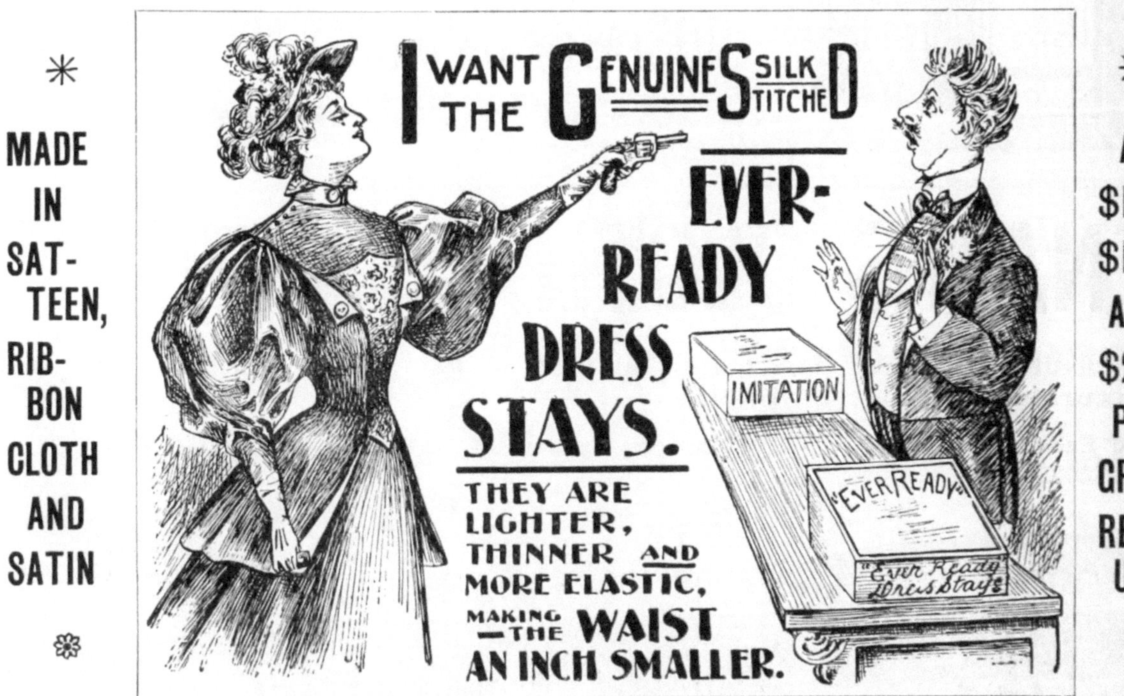

*

AT $1.25, $1.50 AND $2.00 PER GROSS, REGULAR

❋

"THE GENUINE STITCHED EVER-READYS"

The best is none too good for Canadian trade, but if you want a cheaper Dress Stay write us the price and we will supply you.

—— We Want Your Business ——

NEARLY EVERY JOBBER SELLS OUR GOODS

IF YOURS DOES **NOT**, ORDER DIRECT

The EVER-READY DRESS STAY Co'y

WINDSOR - ONTARIO

Brice, Palmer & Co.

MANUFACTURERS

OF

THE CELEBRATED

"EMINENT" Showerproof Cloaks

Largest selection in the trade.

Agents in J. E. SNIDER & CO. 5 King St. West TORONTO Canada

Who have a range of samples for winter, as well as of **Tailor=made Jackets and Capes, Children's Reefers, etc.**

Wholesale and Export, 90, 92, 94 and 96 City Road
Warehouse, 14 Cannon Street

Telegrams,
"Eminent," London

LONDON, ENGLAND

World Wide Popularity   **The Delicious Perfume.**

Crab Apple Blossoms

EXTRA CONCENTRATED

Put up in 1, 2, 3, 4, 6, 8, and 16 ounce bottles.

And the Celebrated

Crown Lavender Salts

Annual sales exceed 500,000 bottles.
Sold everywhere.

THE CROWN PERFUMERY CO.

177 New Bond St., London, Eng.

By all principal dealers in perfumery.

Medals taken at all Exhibitions.

TRADE   MARK

THOS. HEMMING & SON, Ltd.

Manufacturers of

NEEDLES FISH HOOKS and FISHING TACKLE.

WINDSOR MILLS - REDDITCH, ENGLAND.

Write for Samples, which will be mailed to you free on receipt of Trade Card.

THE CELEBRATED OXFORD
FLANNELETTE AND FLANNEL UNDERCLOTHING AND BABY LINEN

W. F. Lucas & Co.

129a London Wall

London, England.

Do You Ask . . .

What's in a Name?

There's a good deal represented in the name of

P.C. CORSETS

—BECAUSE—

When you sell or recommend them they are sure to meet with approval as every detail in their "make-up" is **Perfect.**

—THEIR—

Appearance, Material, Shape, Attractiveness are the most prominent trade-winning features in our various makes.

We would particularly draw your attention to our **"EMPIRE" and "FLORA" Brands** with their **Patent Safety Pockets.** They sell on sight. **Why?** Because they are **"Pre-eminent"** in every sense of the word. Send for full particulars. Orders promptly attended to. Give our travellers a look over.

PARISIAN CORSET CO.,   =   Quebec, Que.

P. S.—The increasing demand for our corsets proves beyond all doubt their immense popularity.

WREYFORD & CO.

Wholesale Men's Furnishers

SEASONABLE LINES IN STOCK.      ROMAIN BUILDING, **TORONTO**

English Dress Shirts.
Celebrated "Facile" Brand $12.00 doz. Fresh delivery—round Cuffs.

Pyjama Suits.
Ceylon, at $15.75, $19.00, $25.00.
Silk, at $37.50.

The Best Line of
Dress Suit Cases in Canada.
SEND FOR PRICE LIST AND SAMPLE.

DOMINION AGENTS FOR:

TRESS & CO., London, Eng. —High-Class— **HATS AND CAPS.** Spring samples received. Latest English and New York shapes. Silks, Felts and Straws. **Our 1901 Spring Silk Hat by mail this week.**	**YOUNG & ROCHESTER** LONDON and LONDONDERRY. *Manufacturers of Shirts, Collars, Neckwear, Dressing Gowns, Pyjamas, Etc.* Full ranges for Spring, 1901, now ready. Special ranges Flannel Outing Suits. If you will not be in Toronto, arrange for our travellers to call on you. Or when in London call at 3 Love Lane, Wood St., London, E.C.	**DR. JAEGER'S SANITARY WOOLEN UNDERWEAR.** For Gentlemen, Ladies and Children. For 15 years the STANDARD OF THE WORLD. For 5 years steadily growing in favor in Canada. UNITED GARMENTS. For all Climates. For all Seasons, FAVORABLE TERMS CAN NOW BE OFFERED TO THE TRADE. **If no agent in your town write us** We do your Advertising and supply Retail Price Lists.

THE . . .

JOHN D. IVEY CO., Limited

Our Travellers are out with their Fall Samples.   Wait until you see them before placing orders.   They will interest you.   We cover the Dominion.

Order anything you require through our Letter-Order Department.

"Brighton"

"Highland"

"Alpine"

Outing Hats

for Midsummer.

They come in Grey and Castor.   The "Highland" and "Brighton" have the new Corrugated Crowns.   Write for sample lot and prices.

"Outing"

THE . . .

JOHN D. IVEY CO.

TORONTO   **MONTREAL**   LIMITED

BEE HIVE
Knitting Wools

MADE BY——

J. & J. BALDWIN, & PARTNERS, Limited, HALIFAX, ENG.

The Oldest Established and Largest Makers of

All kinds of Knitting Wools

KNOWN ALL OVER THE CIVILIZED WORLD

Scotch Fingering	Berlin Fingering	Vest and Silk Vest Wool	
Wheeling	Balmoral Fingering	Lady Betty	Pyrenees
Petticoat Fingering	Merino Fingering	Shetland	Fleecy
Soft Merino	Soft Knitting Wool	Andalusian	Dresden

All of the BEE HIVE Brand, and also Red Letter BB Scotch Fingering.　　Mendings

Especially adapted for Hand and Machine Knitting

We claim that they will knit further and wear longer than any other make.

Wholesale Only ——————Send for Samples.

Agent——

Duncan Bell

MONTREAL and TORONTO

Two Hosiery Specialties:

CARTWRIGHT & WARNERS'

CELEBRATED . . . .

"Squirrel Brand"

HOSIERY and UNDERWEAR.

"Queen" (the leading English ladies' paper) says: "The name of Messrs. Cartwright & Warners enjoys such a long-established reputation for excellence in the manufacture of hosiery and underwear, that an experienced shopper is always ready to accord an appreciative welcome to any of their new productions. As long ago as the Great Exhibition of 1851, the well-known firm was awarded a medal for what was then looked upon as a wonderful achievement in the construction of machine-made hosiery, the woollen combination garment which has since become an indispensable item in most wardrobes. Among their numerous improvements of to-day is the development of a new process known as the 'Premier Finish,' which, applied to woollen hosiery and underwear of all descriptions, renders them not only soft and elastic in texture, but *thoroughly unshrinkable in washing.*"

Combinations, Drawers, Vests, etc., bearing this stamp:

are absolutely unshrinkable.

"Monodye"

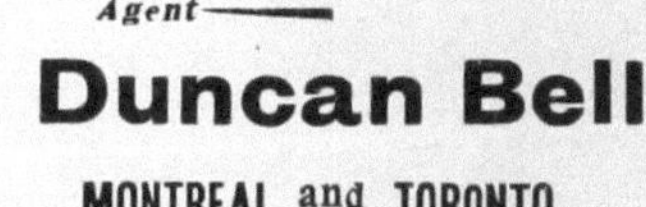

(Registered)

HOSE and HALF-HOSE.

ALL=WOOL—FAST BLACK—
UNSHRINKABLE.

Will not turn green with wear and washing.

"Womanhood," October, 1899, says: "The 'Monodye' Stockings are black all-woollen stockings, in the production of which a great difficulty has been overcome. It has hitherto been found impossible to dye black pure wool stockings in such a way that after repeated washings they do not lose color, most looking quite green after they have been several times through the laundress's hands. The 'Monodye' stockings are, however, perfectly black, and will remain so after any number of washings. They are also quite unshrinkable, and it is a sufficient guarantee of their excellence that they are manufactured by the firm of Cartwright & Warners, one of the oldest-established firms of woollen manufacturers in England. The same firm make the 'Premier Finish' (Squirrel Brand) of all-woollen combination and underwear."

Cartwright & Warners, Limited, Loughborough, England

Canadian Agents: R. FLAWS & SON, Manchester Buildings, Melinda St., TORONTO.

Wholesale Millinery

Sept. 2nd }

We have decided to hold our

FALL OPENING

week commencing —

SEPT. 2nd.

The magnificence of our Display in Trimmed Goods—all lines—will be in keeping with the leading position we hold in the Trade.

We extend a cordial invitation to the Trade of Canada.

THE D. M^CCALL CO., Limited

Smart and Swift

OUR OUTING AND WALKING HATS ARE NOTED FOR . . THEIR "SMART" APPEARANCE AND "SWIFT" SELLING QUALITIES ALL UP-TO-DATE BUYERS WILL TELL YOU SO.

CAVERHILL & KISSOCK

Montreal. Toronto. Ottawa. Quebec.

Spring

JUST

a reminder of the lines our travellers are now showing for

SPRING.

Girls' Wash Dresses in Crash, P K., Percales, etc. —ages 4 to 14 years.

Smart Yoke Effect.

1902

150 styles in Blouses from $6.50 doz. to $7.50 each, in Percales, Madras, Organdy, Sateen, Silk, etc.

25 designs in Print and Muslin House Wrappers from $10 to $24 doz. Wide sweep of skirt, flounced, etc.

Stylish Open Back.

30 smart creations in Wash Skirts, Crash, P.K., Duck, etc.

35 original and up-to-date designs in strictly "tailor-made" cloth costumes, in most artistic effects, from $5 to $35.

Muslin Costumes.

Last season was the first good one. The coming one is sure to be a record-breaker. Don't fail to order liberally of this line or you "won't be in it" when the season opens.

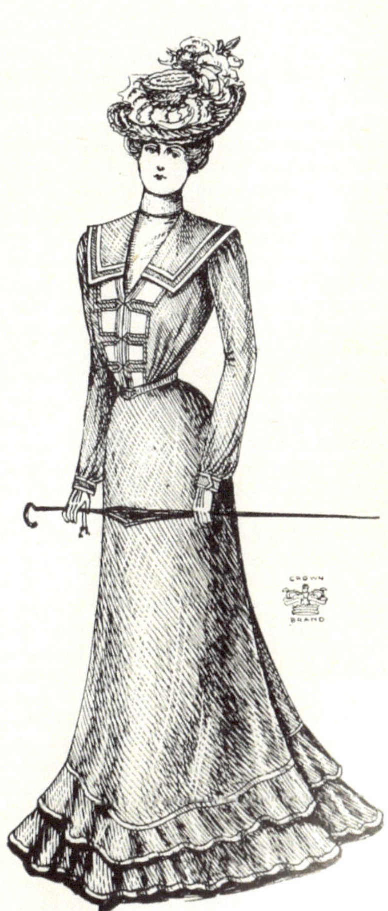

Natty Style in Muslin Costume.

BOULTER & STEWART, Manufacturers, TORONTO.

Fancy Goods
Toys, Dolls
Xmas Novelties
China and Glassware
NEW
CATALOGUE
Now Ready.
Nerlich & Co.
TORONTO.

www.ingramcontent.com/pod-product-compliance
Lightning Source LLC
Chambersburg PA
CBHW042008110726
48006CB00004B/1007